Maaa

by Aunyarat Watanabe

Life is a journey.

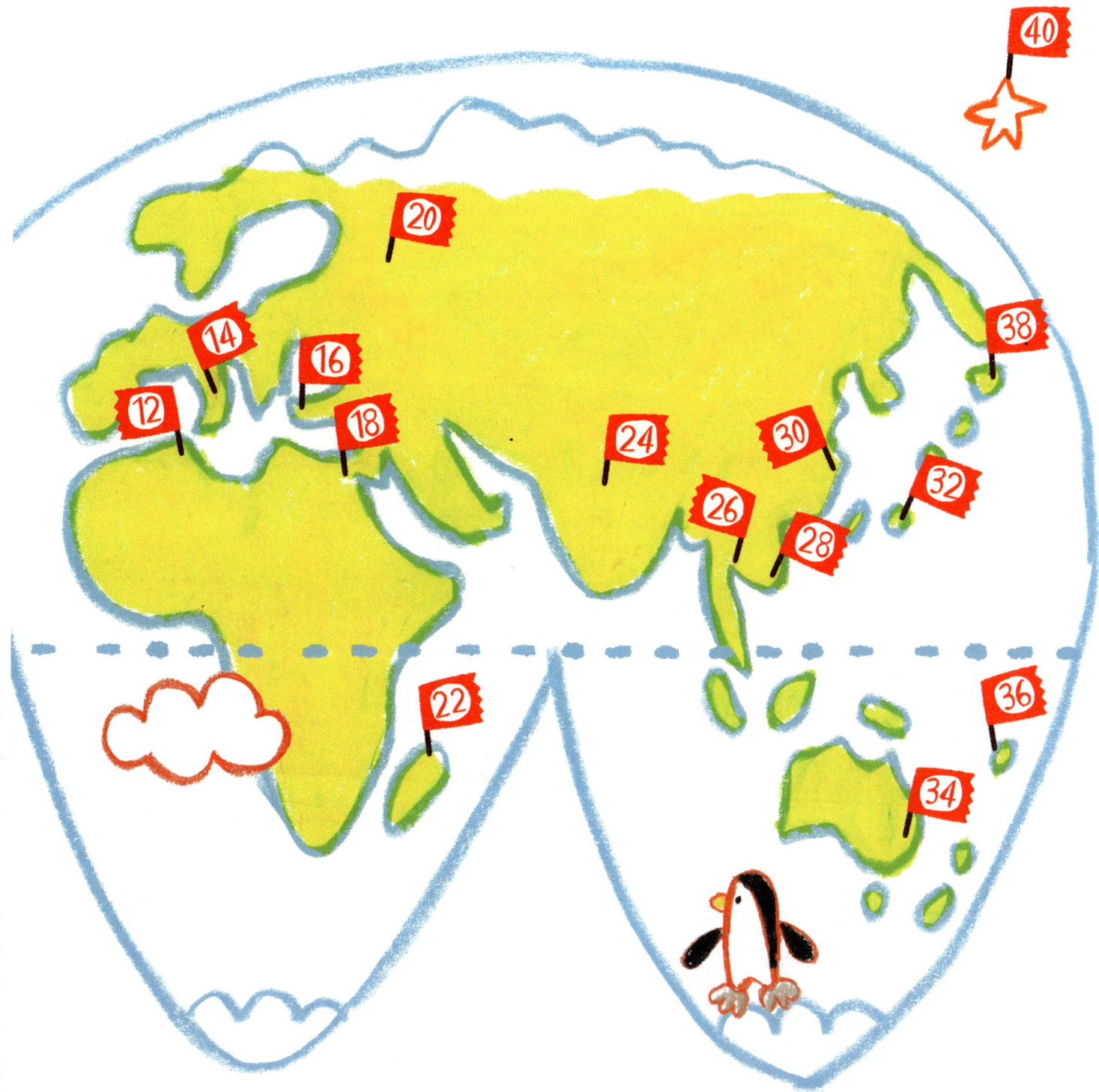

Holo Holo

KAUAI

OAHU

Aloha

THE ISLANDS OF
HAWAII

Do you know what it's like under the bright blue Pacific Ocean? I'll tell you: it's spectacular! Hawaii's marine environment is truly magnificent. If you aren't very comfortable with the bulk of scuba equipment, no worries, you can snorkel or even take a submarine tour!

YUM!

MEXICO CITY

Museo Nacional de Antropología

Avenue Insurgentes Sur

Monumento a la Revolución

Hola!

Tequila

Buenavista St.

Paseo de la Reforma

Avenida Hidalgo

Arameda Park

Mercado!

Catedral Metropolitana

Zócalo

Templo Mayor

Arena Coliseo

Mexico City is vibrant and lively! You can spend hours (or days!) here just browsing the markets, looking at the buildings and enjoying the museums. Don't miss the excitement of Lucha Libre, Mexico's masked wrestlers! On the streets you'll see lots of skeleton Catrina dolls and in the museums you can make friends with the Chac Mools (he's the guy in the upper left corner!).

7

Wow!

The Metropolitan Museum of Art

Rockefeller Center

Chrysler Bldg.

Empire State Bldg

Union Sq.

Yo

American Museum of Natural History

Dakota House

This is one of the most exciting, fun-filled cities in the world. New York City is full of discoveries! It's fun to ride a double-decker bus up Broadway, play frisbee in Central Park, visit the world-famous museums, browse in lovely book shops and eat pizza while walking down the busy sidewalks. Say "hello" to the Statue of Liberty for me!

9

WOW!

Lagoa Rodrigo
de Freitas

Morro do
Corcovado

Praia de
Copacabana

Pão de
Açúcar

Estádio do Maracanã

Central do Brasil

Rio de Janeiro

Sugar Loaf Mountain, known locally as Pão de Açúcar, is a must-see! You can take a cable car there and enjoy breath-taking views along the way. If you are eager to get higher and see a full view of the beautiful coasts, you can even take a helicopter tour. Afterwards it's fun to sit on the beach and watch the locals play volleyball...with their feet!

11

S ⊕ N
100M

Rue Tourbet el Bay

Mosquée Sidi Yousset

Grande Mosquée

Library

Souk el Belat

Mint Tea!!

Rue des Teinturiers

Rue Sidi Ali Azouz

Rue Jamaa ez Zitouna

Bab Bhar

START

Place de La Victoire

12

La Médina de Tunis

Lovely restaurant

Hammam Spa

R. Sidi Ben Arous

Olive onion bread

YUM!

Rue Sidi Mahrez

Souk el Granaa

Meow!

The historic Médina in Tunis is a big maze of winding alleys with many shops and historic buildings. In this awesome place you can buy just about everything: from underwear and carpets to spices, jewels, antiques and so much more. I sat in a little café and drank a fresh mint tea then I bought a fluffy stuffed camel toy and a flying carpet. Wheeee!!!

13

ROMA

CASTEL SANT'ANGELO

GIOLITTI

SANT'EUSTACHIO

PANTHEON

Buono!

ISONA TIBERINA

BOCCA DELLA VERITA

CHIESA DI SAN FRANCESCO A RIPA

14

PIAZZA DI SPAGNA

TERMINI st

BASILICA DI SANTA MARIA MAGGIORE

COLLOSEO

In Rome, your meals go something like this: gelato for breakfast, pizza for lunch, gelato for second lunch, gelato for third lunch, pasta for dinner and gelato for dessert. Heaven! I think I tried every single flavor. Thankfully, Rome is a great city to walk around in all day long so all that gelato gave me the energy to keep going.

15

ISTANBUL

Macar Kardeşler St.

Atatürk Bul.

Istanbul Uni

Grand Bazaar

TAKSI

Golden Horn

Spoonmaker's Diamond

Topkapi Palace

Aya Sofya

Blue Mosque

86 carat!

Pomegranate juice

Mackerel Sandwich

Sea of Marmara

Istanbul is the capital of Turkey and the only one city in the world that straddles two continents. It spans both Europe and Asia. It's exciting to so easily cross over from one continent to another. The Blue Mosque, Hagia Sophia and The Grand Bazaar are amaaaazing! You will be in awe of the majestic architecture and rich history.

17

If you are fascinated with ancient mysteries, Egypt is the place to go! The Pyramids are over 4,500 years old. In the museum you'll see Tutankhamen's golden mask and lots of mummies (cat mummies too!). There are so many things in Egypt that will make you say "Wow!". I especially love the contrast of the beautiful Nile River next to the parched Sahara Desert.

19

MOSCOW

Matryoshka Museum

Kremlin

Library

New Arbat St.

Arbat St.

← Cat Circus

My-My

Pushkin's house

Moskva River

Tretyakov Gallary

20

Bolshoi Theatre

Mayakovsky Museum

Yaroslav Sta.

Saint Basil's Cathedral

Roar!

Siberian Railway

MEOW!

Москва

Saint Basil's Cathedral in Moscow is one of my favorite buildings in the world. It is like the Taj Mahal of Russia. Look at the spiraling onion domes! There are many architectural monuments in Moscow. Even the metro stations look like underground castles—awesome! You can't walk away from Moscow without buying a set (or two) of Matryoshka dolls—soooo cute!

21

MADAGASCAR

←Aye-aye!

Sambava

Ankarana Reserve

Vanilla!

Tomato frog

Mahajanga

Antananarivo

Comet moth ♥

Luuunch!

Kirindy Reserve

Pitcher plant & her lunch

22

Perinet Reserve

CHAMELEON XING

Route 7 941 km

Baobab in LOVE!

Taolagnaro

Berenty Reserve

Toliara

I'm a giraffe beetle

Scientists think the island of Madagascar broke off from Africa about 160 million years ago. Wow! Everything in Madagascar is sooo unique and fun! Chameleons are busy changing their colors, monkeys are jumping around and turtles are hiding in their shells. Even the Baobab trees are in love! If you are lucky, you might encounter an Aye-aye!

24

Banaras

INDIA

Bengaluru

India is a land of mysteries. It is probably the most colorful, crazy, exciting country in the world. There are just so many people! And cows! You can't help but wonder where everyone came from and where they're going. If a bus is full, the locals hang out the door or sit on the roof. Cool! There's a photo opportunity around every corner, so keep your camera handy!

Do you know which city has the longest name? Bangkok!
It's official name (in Thai) is "Krungthepmahanakhon
Amonrattanakosin Mahintharayutthaya Mahadilokphop
Noppharatratchathaniburirom Udomratchaniwetmahasathan
Amonphimanawatansathit Sakkathatiyawitsanukamprasit".
Wow! Can you repeat that for me please!?

27

Xin chao

HO CHI MINH CITY

Water Puppet Theater

N ên Trãi

Lê Lai

Hot stone massage

Notre Dame Cathedral

Post office

Toa Nha ''BND T.P.

Nguyễn Huê

Saigon Opera House

Lê Loi

Pham Hồng Thái

Ben Thanh Market

Hàm Nghi

Sài Gòn River

Ho Chi Minh City in Vietnam is one of the absolute best cities to eat in all of Southeast Asia. Food carts that sell delicious street food can be found everywhere! It's hard for me to choose a favorite, but it's probably banh mi, a Vietnamese sandwich usually made with fresh vegetables, herbs and ham. I love sweet sticky rice, too. Oh, and spring rolls. Yum!

29

CHINESE ACROBAT

YUM!

Changping Rd.

Metro

TAXI

Jing'an Temple

Line ⑦

Changping Rd.

SHANGHAI

ANTIQUE MARKET

Shanghai is a fantastic mix of ancient and traditional with super modern and new. You simply can't get bored exploring this city. I do love snacking on all the street food here too! There are lots of different kinds and they all call my name. How could I say "no" to a juicy pork bun? It goes so well with a yummy bubble milk tea!

OKINAWA

GRRR

IRIOMOTE

ISHIGAKI

Okinawa, in southern Japan, is surrounded by endlessly clear, beautifully blue waters. And the view is even more breathtaking underwater! It's a paradise of marine life: clownfish, butterfly fish, manta rays, and a vast coral reef. If you're lucky, you may even see a whale shark, which is said to be the world's largest fish (remember, a whale is a mammal, not a fish!).

33

STOP

501

SYDNEY OBSERVATORY

CBD

CITY RAIL

Wynyard

MCA

MUSEUM OF CONTEMPORARY ART

CIRCULAR QUAY

SYDNEY

← DARLING HARBOUR

THE WHARF

Jet

VENTUNO BEST PIZZA!

THE ROCKS

PANCAKES ON THE ROCKS

WALSH BAY

MILSONS POINT ⇒

CAPTAIN COOK CRUISE ⇒

MANLY ⇒

HOT CHOCOLATE

DENDY CINEMA

TARONGA ZOO ⇒

My favorite viewpoint in Sydney is that of the Sydney Opera House seen from Harbour Bridge. When night comes, it looks like beautiful white swans floating on the sea. If you want to see some really cool animals, you can take a boat from the harbor to Taronga Zoo. The cute koala bears and crazy kangaroos will be waiting for you!

35

MYSTERY ISLAND

AM11:00

WOODEN COTTAGES

HAPPY COUPLE

BAR

RESTAURANT

BULA!
SPA
TURTLE
NESTING AREA
MYSTERY ISLAND
PM11:00
-FIJI-
HERE
NADI

This small island is one of over 300 islands in Fiji. Mystery Island is surrounded by a beautiful white sand beach and large lagoon. It takes just 7 minutes to walk around the whole island. There are only two cottages in which you can stay, so at nighttime it's your own private island where the only light is from lanterns and the glorious starry sky!!!

Lake
Abashiri

ICE BREAKER SHIP

Abashiri
Sta.

Makoto
Sta.

Northan
peoples
Museum

Kitahama
Sta.

AIR DO

Memanbetsu
Airport

Lake Tofutsu

Norokko Train

OKHOTSK SEA

SHIRETOKO PENINSULA

Siretoko
Shari Sta.

Senmou Line

DRIFT ICE
HOKKAIDO ABASHIRI-SHIRETOKO

Shiretoko is considered the most beautiful of all the national parks in Japan. It's very far north and very few people live up there, but it is the home of a diverse number of animal species, including bears, deer, foxes, eagles and owls! During winter, the Sea of Okhotsk is one of the best places in the world to see the miniature floating icebergs called drift ice. Brrrr!

39

IRON RESTAURANT

PINEAPPLE COMPUTER

TAXI

COOL!

Our solar system is about 4500000000 years old!

Library

Olympus Mons

STAR Univ.

BLACK HOLE THEATRE

TICKET

Mars Language School

Yippee!

Can you imagine what it would be like to live on Mars in 2095? Mars is called the "red planet" because it is covered with a rusty red dust which is actually iron oxide. So, before you leave Earth, be sure to pack tons of soap, laundry detergent and a broom!!

41

42

Here is a place where you can draw your own map of anyplace in the world!

Produced & published by *They Draw & Travel*
Studio SSS, LLC
13 Steepleview Drive
Hudson, Ohio 44236
theydrawandtravel.com

Illustrated & written by Aunyarat Watanabe
watanabe.rocket.ne.jp

Designed & edited by Nate Padavick
studiosss.tumblr.com

23585116R00026

Made in the USA
Charleston, SC
30 October 2013